SUCCESS LEARNING

LEE LEE'S
SUCCESS LEARNING LAB

Name:

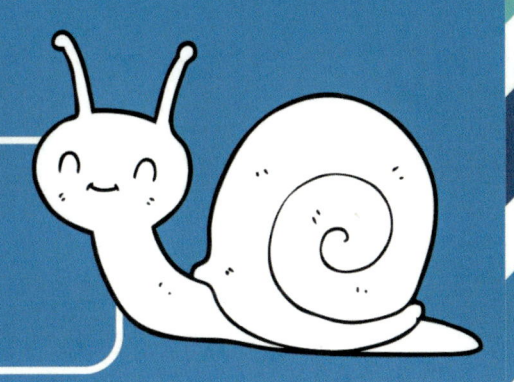

LEE LEE'S
SUCCESS LEARNING LAB

Success Learning Lab 2021 by Aleeyah Henry

All Rights Reserved.
Printed in the United States of America.
For information, address
Lee Lee's Success Learning Lab
www.successlearninglab.com

The Library Of Congress Cataloging in Publication Data
Is available upon request.

ISBN

All Rights Reserved Worldwide. No part of this publication may be reproduced, distributed, or transmitted in any form or by any means, including photocopying, recording scanning, or other electronic or mechanical methods, without the prior written permission of the publisher or author, Aleeyah Henry. Please do not participate in or encourage piracy of copyrighted materials that are in violation of the author's rights.

For more information on purchases in bulk for promotional, educational, business use, or speaking events, please contact Aleeyah Henry, info@successlearninglab.com

LEE LEE'S
SUCCESS LEARNING LAB

In Honor and Memory of my Dad, Claudious Henry

This book is dedicated to all of the students who just want to learn and be the best versions of themselves.

LEE LEE'S
SUCCESS LEARNING LAB

CONNECT WITH US:

@SUCCESSLEARNINGLAB

WWW.SUCCESSLEARNINGLAB.COM

FREE BONUS

Download the ANSWER KEY

Visit:

Answer.successlearninglab.com

Use code "answer" to redeem

LEE LEE'S
SUCCESS LEARNING LAB

Rounding Up to Nearest Thousand

| 3124 | 5587 | 6500 | 8123 | 1035 |
| 3000 | 6000 | ____ | ____ | ____ |

| 6234 | 5986 | 3512 | 4444 | 5897 |
| ____ | ____ | ____ | ____ | ____ |

| 1466 | 6438 | 3545 | 9800 | 7360 |
| ____ | ____ | ____ | ____ | ____ |

| 9652 | 1398 | 5249 | 3822 | 5936 |
| ____ | ____ | ____ | ____ | ____ |

| 4961 | 9872 | 7598 | 6923 | 1267 |
| ____ | ____ | ____ | ____ | ____ |

| 2372 | 5023 | 1134 | 3822 | 1164 |
| ____ | ____ | ____ | ____ | ____ |

Divide the Pizza

Can you help our friends get equal slices?

Compose the division equations with this guide:
Dividend: Number of parts   Divisor: Number of friends   Quotient: Your answer

5 Friends

3 Friends

4 Friends

2 Friends

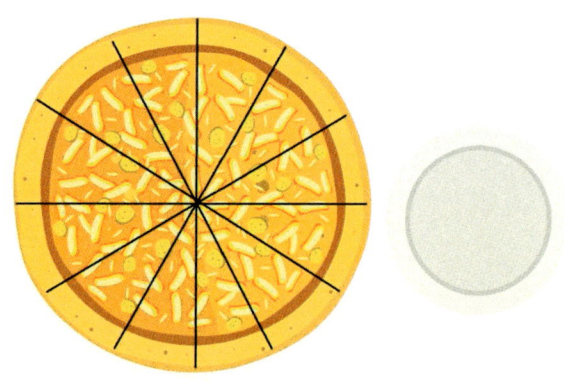

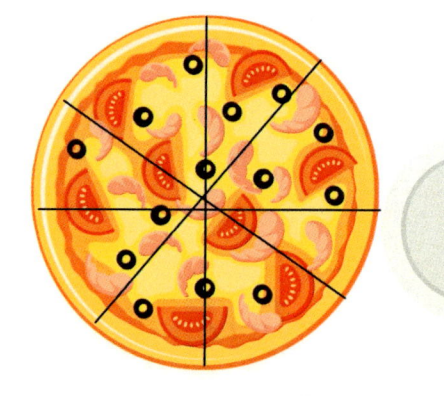

6 Friends

8 Friends

SHOW YOUR WORK

Solve the Addition and Show Your Work Below

Sam has 16 saplings and his sister, Trish has 22 saplings, then how many saplings do they have in total?
Can you tell why we should plant saplings?

TELLING TIME

Draw the hands of the clock by looking at the time below

11:55

Hour ⭘→

Minutes ⭘→

4:05

7:10

10:30

3:15

8:25

2:45

1:05

5:40

Pictorial Division

Look at the pictures and count the number of things in order to solve the sums

Stacy has 32 crayons in total, then how many boxes of crayons did she buy?

Jason has 80 chocolates in total, then how many boxes of chocolates does he have?

Trish bought 78 eggs in toal, how many crates of eggs did she buy?

MULTIPLICATION PRACTICE

```
  54        74        93        79        60        27
x 33      x 25      x 58      x 40      x 31      x 13
----      ----      ----      ----      ----      ----


  55        67        85        70        34        84
x 52      x 43      x 18      x 27      x 43      x 60
----      ----      ----      ----      ----      ----


  96        45        87        66        44        38
x 31      x 27      x 24      x 18      x 35      x 52
----      ----      ----      ----      ----      ----
```

DIVISION

```
      __                           __
42 ) 546                     38 ) 722
    - __                         - __
      ____                         ____
      - __                         - __
       ____                         ____
         0                            0
```

```
      __                           __
52 ) 780                     16 ) 528
    - __                         - __
      ____                         ____
      - __                         - __
       ____                         ____
         0                            0
```

```
      __                           __
26 ) 910                     22 ) 704
    - __                         - __
      ____                         ____
      - __                         - __
       ____                         ____
         0                            0
```

HOLIDAY EQUATIONS

Let's add or subtract to get equal answers on both sides. This way we'll learn how to reach the same answer in different ways.

$3 + 5 = 2 + \underline{6}$

3 + 5 = 8 and 2 + 6 is also equal to 8

$9 - 6 = \underline{8} - 5$

9 - 6 = 3 and 8 - 5 is also equal to 3

$\underline{} - 7 = 8 - 4$

$3 + 6 = \underline{} + 5$

$7 - \underline{} = 9 - 3$

$\underline{} + 4 = 2 + 5$

$3 - 2 = 9 - \underline{}$

$8 + \underline{} = 9 + 3$

$\underline{} - 6 = 7 - 2$

$4 + 8 = \underline{} + 6$

$8 + \underline{} = 2 + 9$

$8 - 5 = 7 - \underline{}$

$\underline{} + 4 = 1 + 6$

$7 - 5 = 8 - \underline{}$

$3 + \underline{} = 4 + 7$

$\underline{} - 6 = 3 - 1$

$2 + 5 = 7 + \underline{}$

$6 - \underline{} = 7 - 1$

SPOOKY EQUATIONS

6 - _2_ = 3 + 1

3 + 5 = 8 - __

9 - __ = 4 + 2

7 + 2 = 9 - __

8 - __ = 4 + 3

3 + 6 = 12 - __

9 - __ = 1 + 4

2 + 9 = 15 - __

4 + 8 = _18_ - 6

__ - 9 = 7 + 3

7 + 4 = __ - 5

__ - 9 = 0 + 1

4 + 5 = __ - 3

__ - 9 = 11 + 2

5 + 9 = __ - 6

__ - 7 = 1 + 5

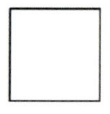

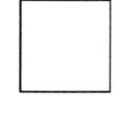

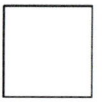

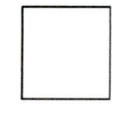

Choose the Correct Answer

a. **2** Even [X] Odd [ ]

b. **7** Even [ ] Odd [ ]

c. **16** Even [ ] Odd [ ]

d. **8** Even [ ] Odd [ ]

e. **213** Even [ ] Odd [ ]

f. **24** Even [ ] Odd [ ]

g. **110** Even [ ] Odd [ ]

h. **9** Even [ ] Odd [ ]

i. **168** Even [ ] Odd [ ]

j. **55** Even [ ] Odd [ ]

k. **96** Even [ ] Odd [ ]

MULTIPLICATION PRACTICE

```
  45        56        71        37        27        82
x 21      x 62      x 36      x 42      x 19      x 20
————      ————      ————      ————      ————      ————


  49        76        95        69        88        53
x 53      x 32      x 48      x 27      x 24      x 65
————      ————      ————      ————      ————      ————


  89        35        19        37        28        43
x 59      x 28      x 26      x 45      x 35      x 47
————      ————      ————      ————      ————      ————
```

SIMPLE DIVISION

Using the first one as your example, complete the following simple division problems.

```
        13
     ┌─────
  13 │ 169
     - 13
     ─────
        39
      - 39
     ─────
         0
```

```
        _ _
     ┌─────
  14 │ 336
      - _ _
     ─────
        _ _
      - _ _
     ─────
         0
```

```
        _ _
     ┌─────
  17 │ 595
      - 
       _ _
     ─────
       _ _
     - _ _
     ─────
         0
```

```
        _ _
     ┌─────
  15 │ 525
      -
       _ _
     ─────
       _ _
     - _ _
     ─────
         0
```

```
        _ _
     ┌─────
  19 │ 494
      -
       _ _
     ─────
       _ _
     - _ _
     ─────
         0
```

```
        _ _
     ┌─────
  18 │ 342
      -
       _ _
     ─────
       _ _
     - _ _
     ─────
         0
```

```
      __                              __
23 | 805                        14 | 672
    __                              __
  - __                            - __
    ‾‾‾‾                            ‾‾‾‾
      __                              __
    - __                            - __
    ‾‾‾‾                            ‾‾‾‾
      0                              0


      __                              __
19 | 608                        13 | 728
    __                              __
  - __                            - __
    ‾‾‾‾                            ‾‾‾‾
      __                              __
    - __                            - __
    ‾‾‾‾                            ‾‾‾‾
      0                              0


      __                              __
16 | 992                        15 | 870
    __                              __
  - __                            - __
    ‾‾‾‾                            ‾‾‾‾
      __                              __
    - __                            - __
    ‾‾‾‾                            ‾‾‾‾
      0                              0
```

DIVISION DRILL
How many equations can you finish in 30 minutes?

Directions: You are given 45 division equations. Solve as many equations as you can in 30 minutes. Answers have no remainders.

1) 48 ÷ 6 =

2) 35 ÷ 5 =

3) 63 ÷ 9 =

4) 35 ÷ 7 =

5) 21 ÷ 3 =

6) 28 ÷ 7 =

7) 40 ÷ 5 =

8) 6 ÷ 2 =

9) 10 ÷ 5 =

10) 63 ÷ 9 =

11) 20 ÷ 2 =

12) 35 ÷ 5 =

13) 8 ÷ 2 =

14) 72 ÷ 8 =

15) 30 ÷ 3 =

16) 90 ÷ 9 =

17) 72 ÷ 9 =

18) 50 ÷ 5 =

19) 24 ÷ 6 =

20) 18 ÷ 9 =

21) 12 ÷ 2 =

22) 48 ÷ 6 =

23) 24 ÷ 3 =

24) 12 ÷ 3 =

25) 18 ÷ 3 =

26) 21 ÷ 7 =

27) 34 ÷ 4 =

28) 36 ÷ 4 =

29) 30 ÷ 10 =

30) 70 ÷ 10 =

31) 81 ÷ 9 =

32) 24 ÷ 8 =

33) 45 ÷ 9 =

34) 9 ÷ 3 =

35) 12 ÷ 4 =

36) 60 ÷ 6 =

37) 4 ÷ 2 =

38) 60 ÷ 10 =

39) 14 ÷ 7 =

40) 10 ÷ 2 =

41) 15 ÷ 5 =

42) 49 ÷ 7 =

43) 8 ÷ 4 =

44) 24 ÷ 4 =

45) 63 ÷ 7 =

SPOOKY MATH CHALLENGE

How fast can you escape the castle?

The castle is haunted by unsolved equations! Find your way out and get rid of the bats and ghouls by solving each problem.

(36 ÷ 9) - (6 ÷ 2) =

(63 ÷ 7) + (5 X 6) =

(77 ÷ 11) + (16 ÷ 4) =

(15 X 5) - (108 ÷ 9) =

(25 X 2) ÷ (80 ÷ 40) =

TURKEY DAY DINNER DASH

Plan Your Thanksgiving Dinner

An Apple Pie costs $6.20, you have 8 family members and each pie serves 2 people, how much will you be spending on Apple Pies?

You have invited 7 guests for Thanksgiving Dinner, but you have only 28 serving bowls, then how many bowls can be served to each guest?

Mental Maths 1

1. How many tens are there in 180 ? _____18_____

2. What is 5 times 13 ? _____

3. What is the remainder when 33 is divided by 5 ? _____

4. A train journey takes 1 hr 30 mins, if I set off at 9:30 am, when will I reach there ? _____

5. Which of these numbers is not even ?
   12   28   56   32   47   60   _____

6. What is 56 – 28 ? _____

7. If an apple costs 21¢, then how much will 3 apples cost ?
   _____

8. What is the double of 25 ? _____

9. How many groups of 4 make 20 ? _____

10. What is the missing number in this sequence ?
    2   5   8   11   14   17   _____

Let's do addition!

514 265 + 123 ――― 902	268 634 + 543 ―――	189 752 + 416 ―――	268 634 + 543 ―――
191 458 +394 ―――	208 873 + 343 ―――	152 308 + 753 ―――	287 124 + 640 ―――
719 935 +444 ―――	850 634 +327 ―――	651 273 +223 ―――	184 458 +394 ―――

SHOW YOUR WORK

Time to do subtraction!

8459	5551	5487	6541
- 7162	- 3990	- 4818	- 6530
1297			

| 8739 | 9514 | 8362 | 1538 |
| - 5421 | - 4687 | - 7157 | - 1290 |

| 7834 | 3510 | 8927 | 9850 |
| - 2800 | - 1658 | - 6348 | - 9725 |

| 6975 | 7560 | 8857 | 5879 |
| - 4390 | - 2930 | - 6510 | - 3306 |

| 3125 | 8432 | 9758 | 1052 |
| - 4612 | - 1906 | - 5946 | - 678 |

SHOW YOUR WORK

FRACTION WALL

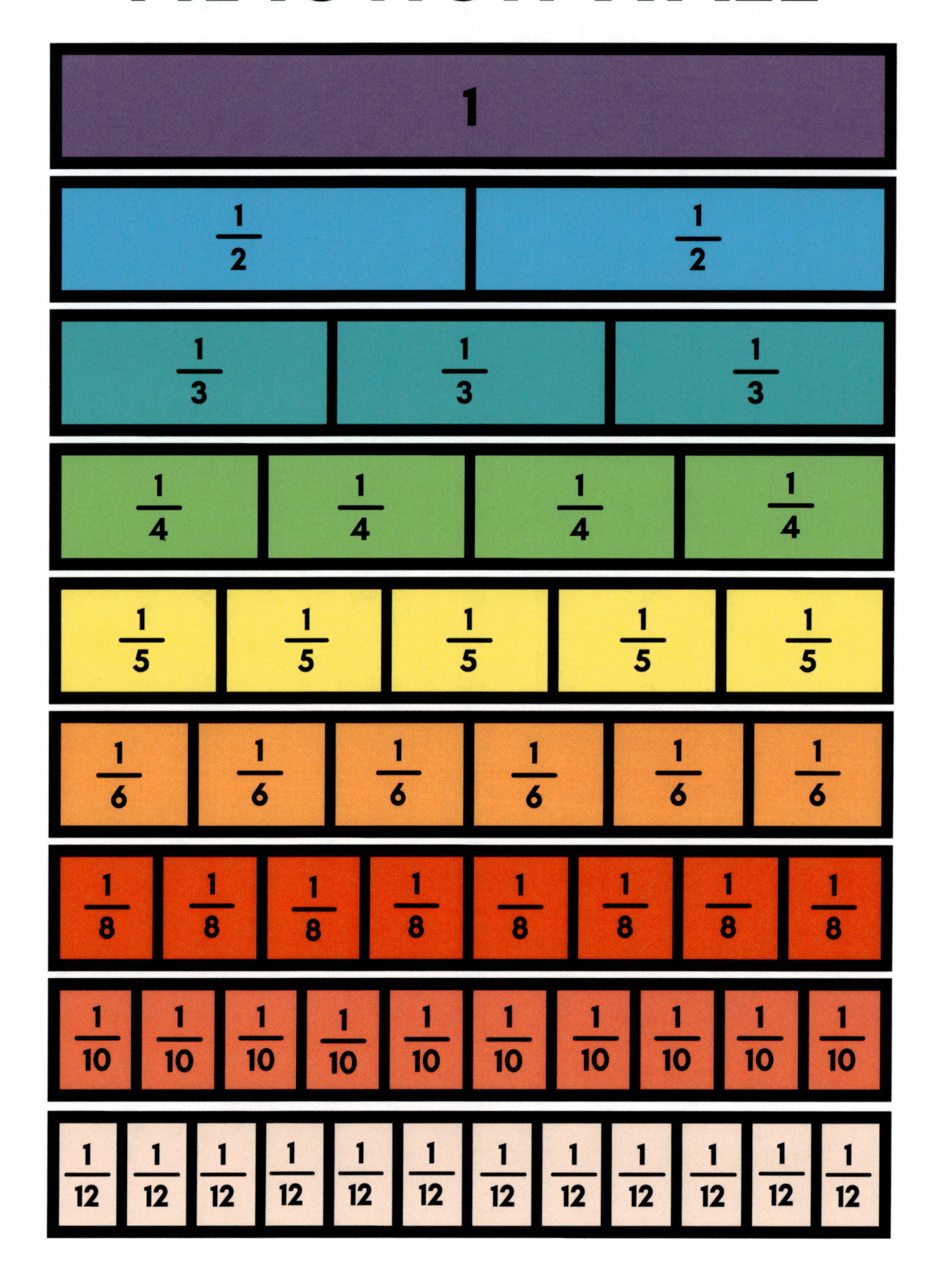

1

| 1/2 | 1/2 |

| 1/3 | 1/3 | 1/3 |

| 1/4 | 1/4 | 1/4 | 1/4 |

| 1/5 | 1/5 | 1/5 | 1/5 | 1/5 |

| 1/6 | 1/6 | 1/6 | 1/6 | 1/6 | 1/6 |

| 1/8 | 1/8 | 1/8 | 1/8 | 1/8 | 1/8 | 1/8 | 1/8 |

| 1/10 | 1/10 | 1/10 | 1/10 | 1/10 | 1/10 | 1/10 | 1/10 | 1/10 | 1/10 |

| 1/12 | 1/12 | 1/12 | 1/12 | 1/12 | 1/12 | 1/12 | 1/12 | 1/12 | 1/12 | 1/12 | 1/12 |

Fractions

1 Shade one half of each shape:

2 Circle shapes that show half:

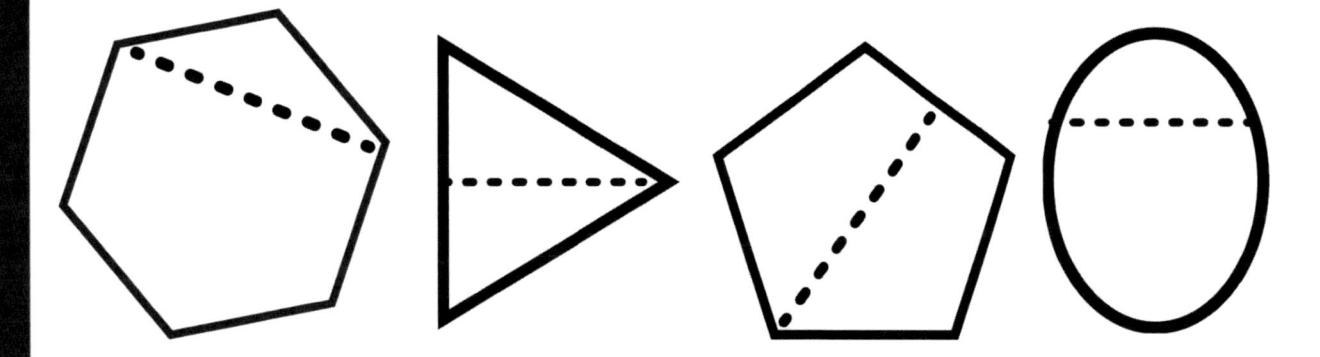

3 Using a ruler, draw lines to make halves of each shape:

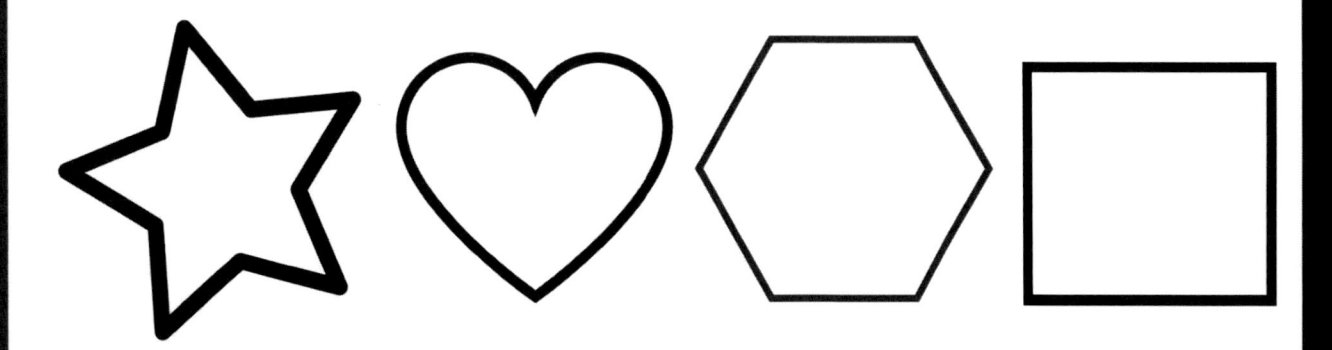

SIMPLIFY THE FOLLOWING

$\dfrac{12}{18} =$ $\dfrac{2}{3}$ $\dfrac{3}{9} =$ $\dfrac{21}{35} =$

$\dfrac{10}{50} =$ $\dfrac{2}{4} =$ $\dfrac{10}{25} =$

$\dfrac{8}{16} =$ $\dfrac{9}{27} =$ $\dfrac{14}{56} =$

$\dfrac{5}{20} =$ $\dfrac{4}{16} =$ $\dfrac{12}{48} =$

$\dfrac{13}{39} =$ $\dfrac{18}{54} =$ $\dfrac{24}{40} =$

Fraction Additions

Look at the pictures in the box given below, each of them indicate a fraction. Solve the equations with the help of the box.

● = 1   ◓ = 1/3   ◐ = 1/2   ◔ = 1/4

1 ● + ● + ◐ = _____

2 ◓ + ◔ + ◐ = _____

3 ◔ + ◔ + ◔ = _____

4 ◐ + ● + ◐ = _____

5 ◓ + ◓ + ◓ + ◔ = _____

6 ● + ◔ + ● + ◓ + ◐ = _____

Fraction Subtraction

Look at the pictures in the box given below, each of them indicate a fraction. Solve the equations with the help of the box.

| ● = 1 | ◓ = 1/3 | ◐ = 1/2 | ◔ = 1/4 |

1. ● + ◔ − ◐ = _____

2. ● − ◓ − ◐ = _____

3. ◐ + ◐ − ◔ = _____

4. ● + ◔ − ◓ = _____

5. ◐ + ◓ − ◔ + ◓ = _____

6. ● − ◔ + ◔ − ◓ + ◐ = _____

Fraction Addition

Add the fractions by finding out the L.C.M. of the denominators

$\frac{3}{5} + \frac{2}{3} =$ $\frac{19}{15}$ $\qquad$ $\frac{1}{2} + \frac{3}{4} =$

$\frac{2}{4} + \frac{2}{5} =$ $\qquad$ $\frac{9}{10} + \frac{1}{2} =$

$\frac{3}{5} + \frac{6}{15} =$ $\qquad$ $\frac{1}{5} + \frac{2}{4} =$

$\frac{8}{10} + \frac{2}{3} =$ $\qquad$ $\frac{4}{5} + \frac{1}{3} =$

$\frac{2}{9} + \frac{3}{6} =$ $\qquad$ $\frac{3}{7} + \frac{6}{14} =$

$\frac{2}{12} + \frac{3}{18} =$ $\qquad$ $\frac{4}{5} + \frac{5}{10} =$

Fraction Subtraction

Subtract the fractions by finding out the L.C.M. of the denominators

$\dfrac{5}{10} - \dfrac{4}{5} =$ $\dfrac{6}{10}$ $\dfrac{4}{6} - \dfrac{1}{8} =$

$\dfrac{7}{9} - \dfrac{3}{6} =$ $\dfrac{2}{5} - \dfrac{2}{6} =$

$\dfrac{9}{10} - \dfrac{4}{5} =$ $\dfrac{4}{12} - \dfrac{3}{9} =$

$\dfrac{3}{5} - \dfrac{1}{7} =$ $\dfrac{4}{8} - \dfrac{2}{12} =$

$\dfrac{8}{10} - \dfrac{2}{3} =$ $\dfrac{1}{4} - \dfrac{1}{5} =$

$\dfrac{2}{3} - \dfrac{5}{10} =$ $\dfrac{3}{4} - \dfrac{2}{10} =$

Multiplying Fractions

Multiply each set of fractions and write your answer in the box below. Make sure to simplify your answer.

$\dfrac{2}{6} \times \dfrac{3}{14}$

$\dfrac{1}{14}$

$\dfrac{1}{12} \times \dfrac{6}{8}$

$\dfrac{25}{7} \times \dfrac{8}{5}$

$\dfrac{8}{3} \times \dfrac{18}{8}$

$\dfrac{3}{7} \times \dfrac{18}{9}$

$\dfrac{26}{13} \times \dfrac{3}{11}$

$\dfrac{12}{21} \times \dfrac{7}{48}$

$\dfrac{11}{1} \times \dfrac{9}{33}$

$\dfrac{20}{35} \times \dfrac{5}{4}$

$\dfrac{2}{8} \times \dfrac{64}{16}$

$\dfrac{5}{18} \times \dfrac{9}{1}$

Dividing Fractions

Divide each set of fractions and write your answer in the box below. Make sure to simplify your answer.

$$\frac{3}{4} \div \frac{9}{16}$$

$$\frac{4}{3}$$

$$\frac{6}{24} \div \frac{4}{10}$$

$$\frac{10}{7} \div \frac{5}{14}$$

$$\frac{9}{5} \div \frac{15}{9}$$

$$\frac{7}{3} \div \frac{20}{32}$$

$$\frac{11}{1} \div \frac{6}{9}$$

$$\frac{3}{9} \div \frac{5}{21}$$

$$\frac{24}{1} \div \frac{4}{25}$$

$$\frac{20}{18} \div \frac{5}{2}$$

$$\frac{11}{12} \div \frac{14}{3}$$

$$\frac{9}{3} \div \frac{2}{1}$$

Adding Decimals

Find the sum of each set of decimals.

4.2 + 3.5

7.7

1.6 + 2.8

8.0 + 5.8

8.5 + 7.2

7.9 + 9.7

14.4 + 16.6

21.6 + 17.4

25.8 + 13.9

20.1 + 34.7

34.50 + 1.2

0.9 + 3.49

13.09 + 9.23

Subtracting Decimals

Find the result of each set of decimals.

0.8 − 0.3

0.5

3.7 − 1.6

7.9 − 7.8

9.9 − 4.4

5.6 − 2.3

14.8 − 10.6

11.9 − 7.4

23.4 − 15.1

20.1 − 14.1

19.8 − 15.0

7.6 − 3.14

13.09 − 9.02

Fractions to Decimals

Convert each fraction to its decimal form. If the decimal is a repeating decimal, make sure to include the vinculum in your answer.

$\dfrac{1}{2}$ = 0.5 $\dfrac{1}{5}$ = $\dfrac{1}{4}$ =

$\dfrac{2}{5}$ = $\dfrac{1}{3}$ = $\dfrac{4}{5}$ =

$\dfrac{2}{3}$ = $\dfrac{9}{10}$ = $\dfrac{1}{8}$ =

$\dfrac{1}{9}$ = $\dfrac{5}{8}$ = $\dfrac{1}{9}$ =

Mental Maths 2

1. What is 1/3 of 21 ? _____7_____

2. Write the missing number 4832 = 4032 + _____

3. Add together 6.5 + 5 + 3.4 _____

4. A bus journey takes 2hr 20 mins, if I set off at 7:15 pm, when will I reach the destination ? _____

5. Which of these numbers is not divisible by 7 ?
   21 35 54 42 77 63   _____

6. What is 42 divided by 6 ? _____

7. If an pen costs $2.70, then how much will 2 pens cost ?
   _____

8. What is the squar of 12 ? _____

9. Write down all the factors of 60 ? _____

10. Write down 5:40 as a 24 hour clock time _____

MATCH THE FOLLOWING

Draw a line to match the food each animal eats

Name a carnivore, a herbivore and an omnivore animal

_____   _____   _____

Fill in the Blanks

FILL IN THE BLANKS WITH THE CORRECT ANSWERS

Food   Air   Water   Shelter
Sunlight   Carbon Dioxide

1. All living things need _____ to drink.

2. All living things need _____ to eat.

3. All living things require _____ to live in.

4. All plants require _____ to grow.

5. All living things need to breathe _____ .

6. All living things exhale _____ when breathing.

List 5 Living Things you can see around you

_____   _____   _____

_____   _____

ANIMAL KINGDOM

Classify the different animals into mammals, birds, fishes, reptiles, amphibians and insects!

_____

_____

_____

_____

_____

ANIMAL KINGDOM

Classify the different animals into mammals, birds, fishes, reptiles, amphibians and insects!

_____

_____

_____

_____

_____

ANIMAL KINGDOM

Classify the different animals into mammals, birds, fishes, reptiles, amphibians and insects!

_____

_____

_____

_____

_____

PLANT FEATURES

Instructions: Draw a plant showing all the parts given in the box below

fruit   bud   trunk   seed
root   flower   branch   leaf

What are things made of ?

Match the following raw materials with the products they are used to make

Tell whether each is a solid, liquid or gas

Oil - _____

Brick - _____

Paint - _____

Sand - _____

Gasoline - _____

Water Vapour - _____

Ice cube - _____

Helium - _____

Shampoo - _____

Popsicle - _____

Smoothie - _____

Oxygen - _____

Cookie - _____

Milk - _____

Planet Scramble

Unscramble the letters, write the word down and connect to the correct Planet

RASM	MARS
TSURNA	
ERHAT	
TPIRJEU	
ENUNEPT	
NUAUSR	
ERRMCYU	
ENVSU	

WILL IT SINK OR FLOAT ?

Let's look at the objects below and guess if they will sink or float

Sink		

Solar System Crossword

Answer the questions below by filling in the blanks in the puzzle.

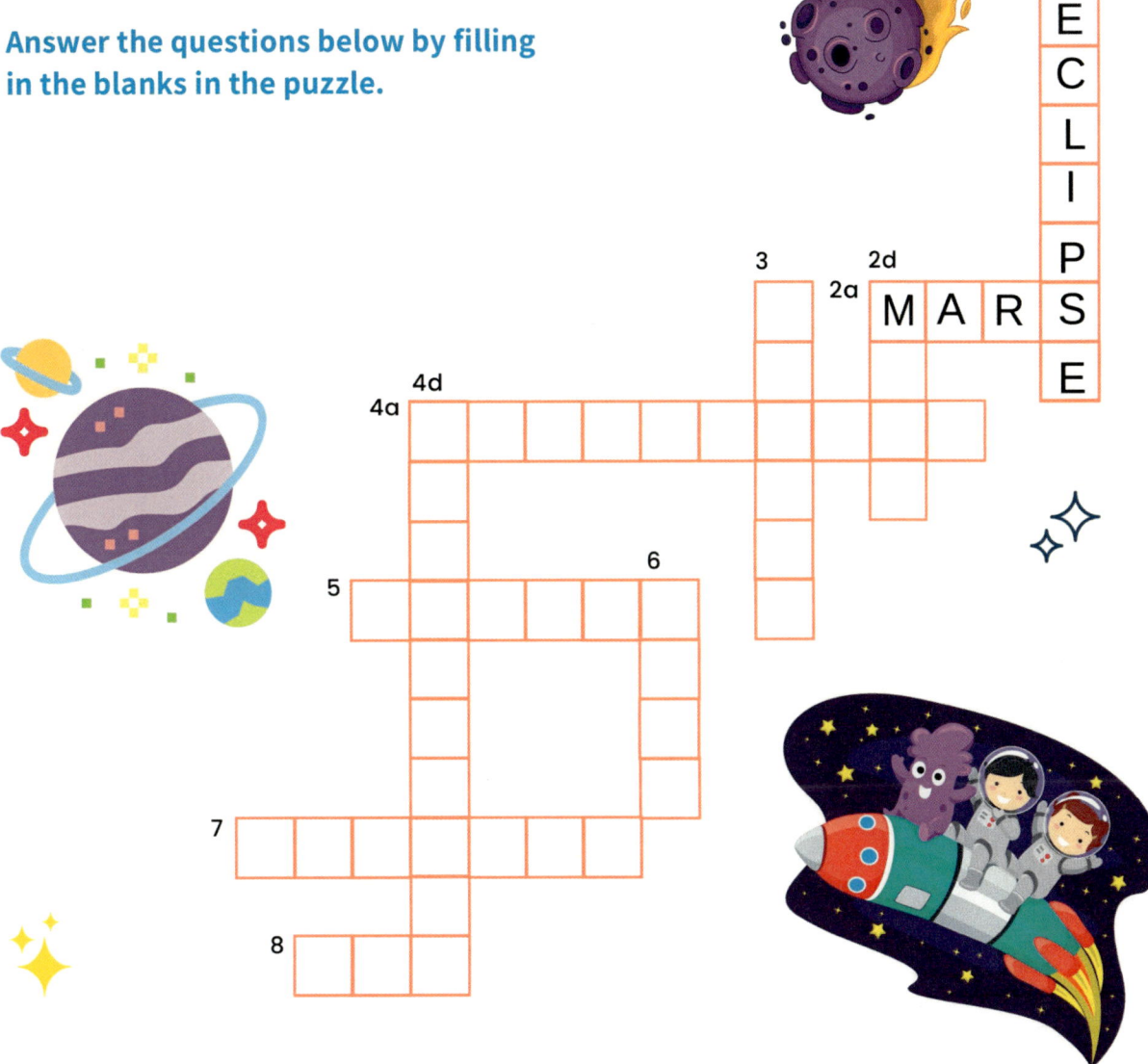

1 down: E C L I P S E

2a: M A R S

ACROSS

- 2a - The planet with the moons Phobos & Deimos.
- 4a - What the moon's light is caused by?
- 5 - Objects that are commonly made of snow, ice, and dust, and can be found moving around outer space.
- 7 - The planet famous for its red spot.
- 8 - The center of our solar system.

DOWN

- 1 - What occurs when one heavenly body (moon or planet) moves into the shadow of another?
- 2d - This is Earth's satellite.
- 3 - The planet that has the most number of rings.
- 4d - One turn around the sun that equals 365 days is called?
- 6 - What is the sun?

PLANT LIFE CYCLE

Instructions: Write number 1 to 6 to show the correct order of the plant's life cycle. Don't forget to label each step!

How does a plant get into this form?

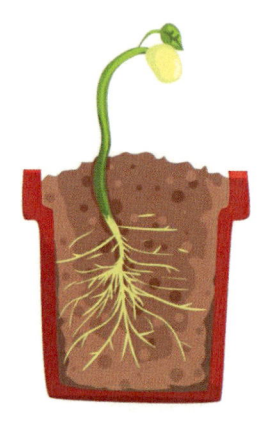

HOW TO PLANT A SEED ?

Instructions: Fill in the blanks with the correct words by looking at the hints given beside each blank!

Follow the steps below to plant a seed

Place some _____ into a _____

Make a _____ with your _____

Drop some _____ into the _____

Cover the _____ with some _____

Pour some _____ into the _____

Give your _____ lots of _____

Wait for your new _____ to grow.

Now perform the steps mentioned above to grow a plant

THE SEED I PLANTED

Instructions: Paste some pictures of the plant which you grew by following the steps before at different stages of its growth

FOOD CHAINS

Rearrange the following food chains in the correct order using arrows!

FOOD CHAINS

Rearrange the following food chains in the correct order using arrows!

ANIMAL KINGDOM

Classify the different animals into reptiles, aves, invertebrates and pisces!

_____

_____

_____

_____

TYPES OF ROCKS

Write short notes on the different types of rocks?

Sedimentary Rock

_____
_____
_____
_____

_____
_____
_____
_____

Igneous Rock

_____
_____
_____
_____

Metamorphic Rock

Types of Pollution and their Causes

Write the causes of various types of pollutions

What are the causes of air pollution?

- _____
- _____
- _____

What are the causes of water pollution?

- _____
- _____
- _____

The presence of or introduction into the environment of a substance which has harmful or poisonous effects.

Types of Pollution and their Causes

Write the causes of various types of pollutions

What are the causes of soil pollution ?

What are the causes of noise pollution ?

The presence of or introduction into the environment of a substance which has harmful or poisonous effects.

SPACE TRIVIA

Let's test your knowledge about Space. Read each question carefully and select the correct answer.

The closest planet to the sun is?

Jupiter   Earth   Mercury   Uranus

Which planet is the least dense in the Solar System?

Saturn   Venus   Jupiter   Neptune

Which planet is named after the ancient Roman god of war?

Mars   Earth   Venus   Saturn

Which planet is the brightest natural object in Earth's night sky after the Moon?

Saturn   Venus   Neptune   Jupiter

The fastest spinning planet in our solar system is?

Mars   Jupiter   Mercury   Uranus

The most distant planet from the sun is?

Neptune   Uranus   Mars   Earth

Photosynthesis

Photosynthesis is the process where plants transform light energy into chemical energy. Plants use this energy to make their own food. The light energy they captured is used to convert carbon dioxide, water, and minerals into oxygen.

Chlorophyll

The pigment that gives plants their green color and helps in the process of photosynthesis.

Did you know?

There are organisms other than plants that can undergo photosynthesis. These include algae and the emerald green sea slug.

The Photosynthesis Process

Plants take in water and carbon dioxide and use energy from the sun to turn them into food.

Within the plant cell, water is oxidized, loses electrons, and is changed into oxygen.

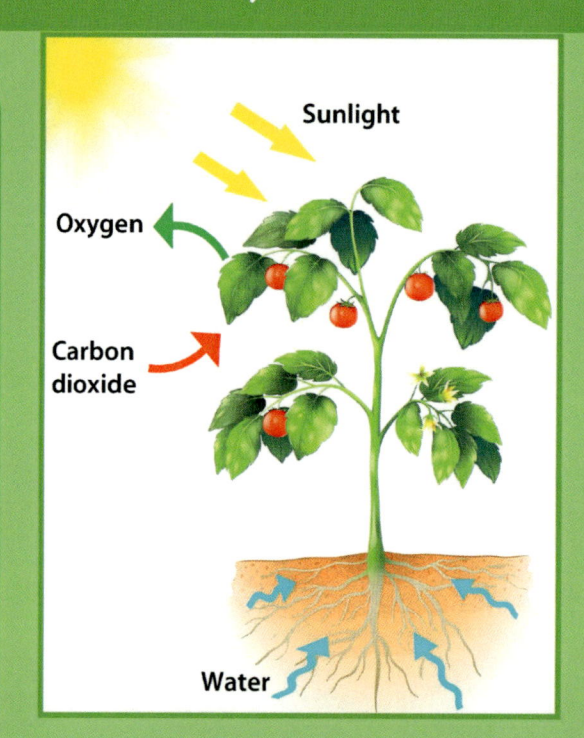

Carbon dioxide is reduced, gains electrons, and turns into glucose.

Oxygen is released, and glucose is stored within the plant as energy.

LIVING THINGS | PLANT FOOD

What are the different parts of the plant which we can eat?

Instructions:
Humans eat many parts of plants like fruits, seeds, stems, roots and leaves. Identify from the pictures below which edible part of plant it is.

STEM
SEED
FRUIT
ROOTS
LEAVES

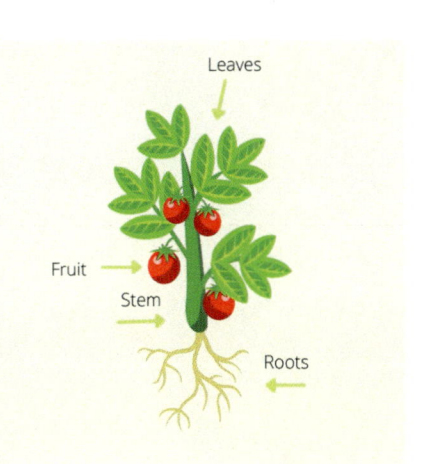

SEED

THE FOOD WEB

Animals in an ecosystem form a food web. In the illustration below, use arrows to map out the energy transfer between organisms. The first one has been added as an example.

Name two producers in the food web above.

_____
_____
_____

Name three consumers in the food web above.

_____
_____
_____

What is the difference between food chains and food webs?

_____
_____
_____

BODY ORGANS

Instructions: Match the functions to each organ.

- Helps us breathe by taking oxygen in, and sending carbon dioxide out.

- Takes waste out of the blood and makes urine.

- A small and large part that absorbs food and water, and excretes waste.

- Pumps blood around the body to keep us alive.

- Digests food.

- Cleans our blood, produces bile, and stores sugar.

- The control centre for speech, coordination, memory, thoughts and emotions.

- Stores and releases urine.

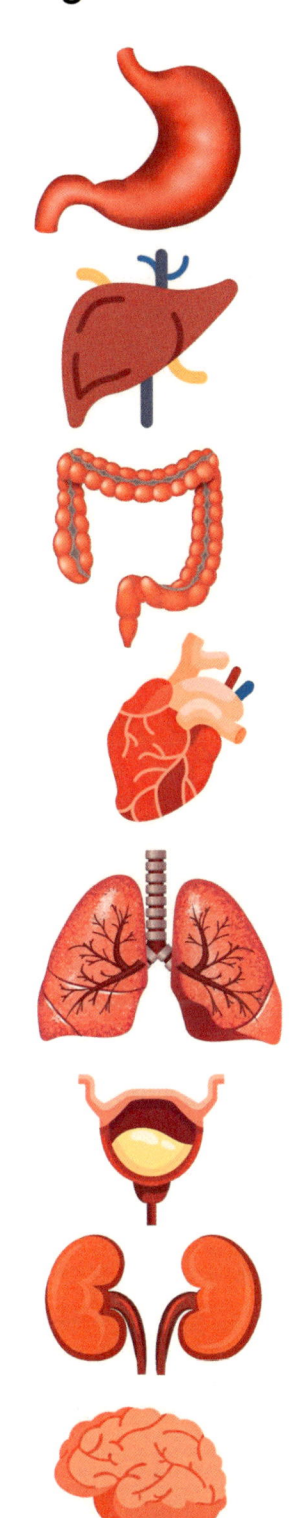

Label the Dancing Skeleton

LABEL THE DIFFERENT PARTS OF THE SKELETON WITH THE WORDS GIVEN IN THE BOX

```
foot bone      hip bone      backbone      knee bone
neck bone      leg bone      thigh bone    skull      ribs
```

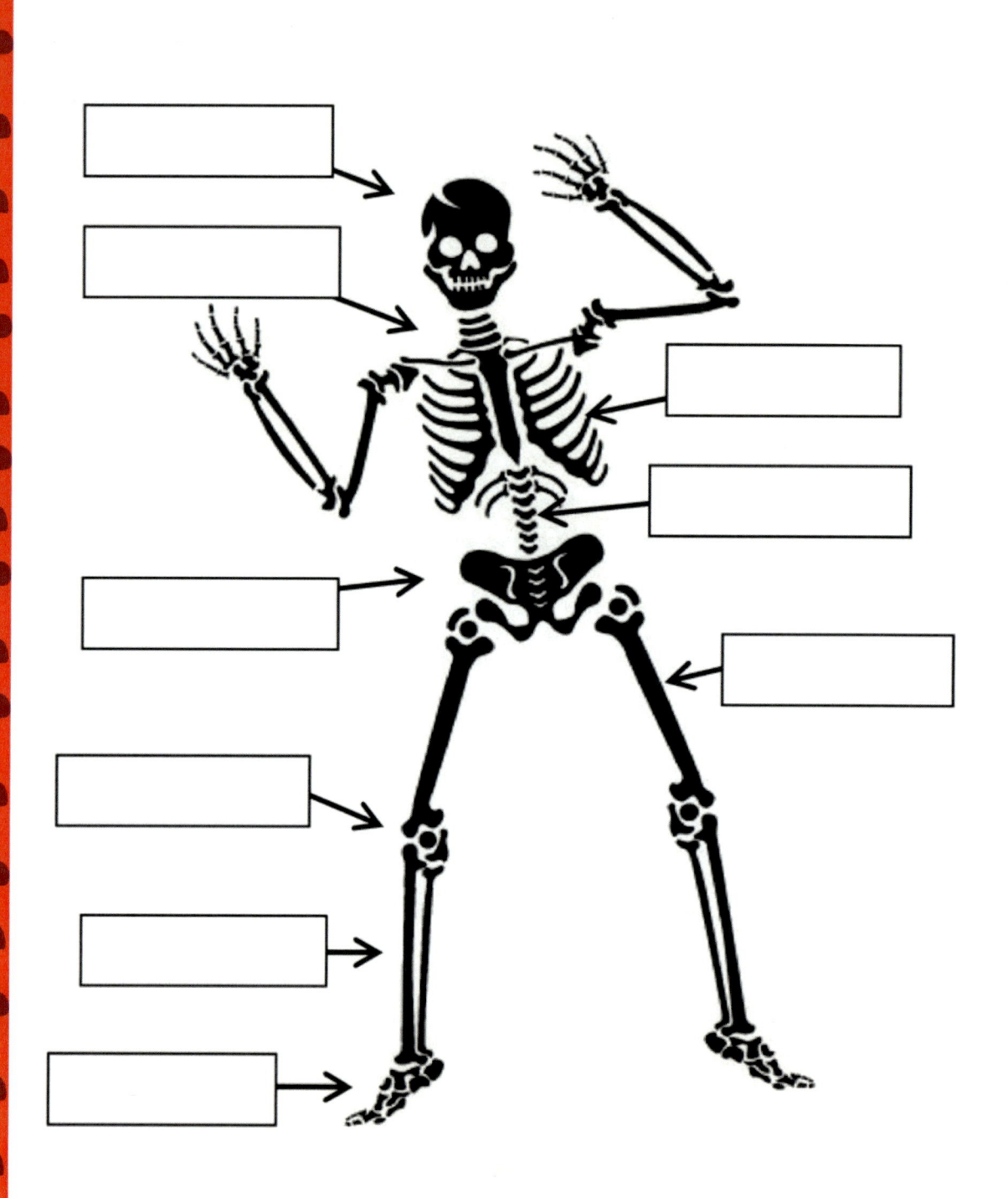

MUSCULAR SYSTEM

FILL IN THE BLANKS WITH THE CORRECT ANSWERS

1. Muscles are connected to bones by _____

   Tendons   Ligaments   Joints

2. _____ muscles are only found in the heart.

   Involuntary   Cardiac   Smooth

3. Muscles which are not under our control are called _____ muscles.

   Voluntary   Involuntary   Skeletal

4. Muscles contracting and relaxing is how we _____

   Sing   Sleep   Move

5. The three types of muscles are cardiac, smooth and _____

   Skeleton   Heart   Tendons

DIGESTIVE SYSTEM

ORGANS INVOLVED IN DIGESTION

CIRCLE ALL THE ORGANS INVOLVED IN DIGESTION

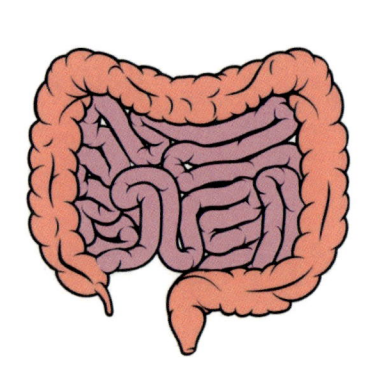

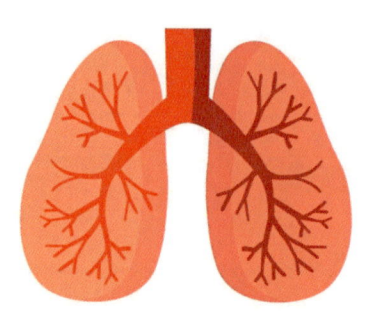

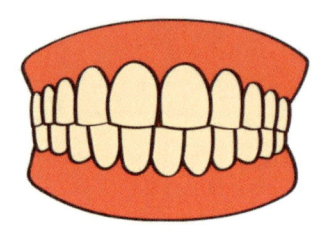

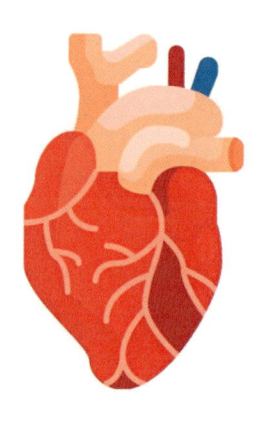

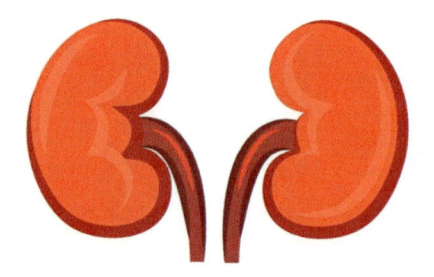

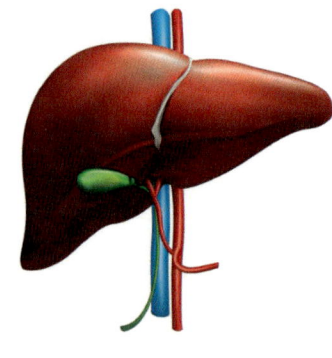

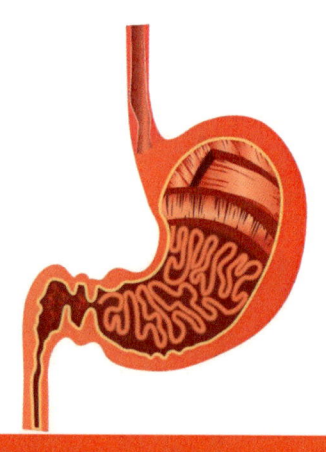

DIGESTIVE SYSTEM

FILL IN THE BLANKS WITH THE CORRECT ANSWERS

1. The _____ breaks down the food we eat.

2. The _____ long narrow tube that has spongy walls soaking up the nutrition from food.

3. A liquid called _____ makes the food wet and soft hence easily digestable.

4. Digestion begins in the _____ when we chew and swallow.

5. The _____ is on the right side of the body, near the lowest rib, its job is to clean the blood.

6. All living organisms produce _____ once digestion is done.

Fill in the blanks with the words given

Waste   Teeth   Liver

Mouth   Bile   Intestine

Different Types of Landforms

Look at the pictures below and identify what kind of landform it is

HINTS

Hills   Plataeu   Desert   Island   Canyon

Volcano   Plain   Jungle   Mountain

Tell whether each set of magnets will attract or repel

_____

_____

_____

_____

_____

SCIENCE QUIZ

TICK THE CORRECT ANSWER FOR EACH OF THE QUESTIONS BELOW

1. What is the pigment that green leaves contain?

    Chlorophyll　　　　Carotenoid　　　　Xanthophyll

2. Which gas produced by plants is useful to us?

    Carbon dioxide　　　　Nitrogen　　　　Oxygen

3. Which one of these is not produced from plants?

    Paper　　　　Leather　　　　Wood

4. What is the smallest planet in our solar system?

    Uranus　　　　Pluto　　　　Neptune

5. Which one is a non renewable source of energy?

    Water　　　　Solar　　　　Fossil Fuel

6. What is our skeleton is covered with?

    Nerves　　　　Tendons　　　　Muscles

7. What kind of animal eats both meat and grass?

    Omnivore　　　　Herbivore　　　　Carnnivore

QUIZ ON METALS

TICK THE CORRECT ANSWER FOR EACH OF THE QUESTIONS BELOW

1. Which metal is used to make jewellery?

    Gold   Iron   Alluminium

2. Which one of these is a liquid metal ?

    Copper   Silver   Mercury

3. Which one of these is a shiny metal?

    Iron   Magnesium   Lead

4. What are metals goos at conducting?

    Heat   Air   Water

5. Which one of these is not a metal ?

    Bromine   Rubber   Copper

6. Iron is not used to make which one of these?

    Coal   Cookware   Steel

7. What is the most common metal found on earth?

    Magnesium   Iron   Silver

CONGRATULATIONS!!!

You have completed the
Success Learning Lab Workbook

Schedule a 1:1 20-min complimentary session to assess your next educational steps.

book.successlearninglab.com

FREE BONUS

Download the ANSWER KEY

Visit:

Answer.successlearninglab.com

Use code "answer" to redeem

ALEEYAH HENRY
Success Learning Lab CEO

Aleeyah Henry was born and raised in the Bronx, New York. She earned her Bachelors' Degree in Computer Information Systems and became a teaching assistant in math at Beacon College in Florida. Aleeyah's gift with math has provided her with the opportunity to expand and enhance her skill set while delving deeper into the realm of science. It wasn't always easy, and she admits to struggling with math in grade school.

This awakening provided Aleeyah with a new direction. She has become a successful business owner and entrepreneur who focuses on helping others improve their math and science skills. Student success and connection are her top priority and she treats each new client with personal interest. The biggest part of her business stems from her investment in the student's progression, providing high level of service, and exceeding expectations. Aleeyah considers the measure of true success when others spread the word for her. Recommendations from others are the highest compliment she can have.

Download your complimentary worksheet @ www.visitourlearninglab.com

Connect with Aleeyah Henry:

Website: www.successlearninglab.com
Instagram: www.instagram.com/successlearninglab

Made in the USA
Middletown, DE
02 March 2024